You Can't Have Everything

You Can't Have Everything

RICHARD SHELTON

UNIVERSITY OF PITTSBURGH PRESS

For Lois

Library of Congress Cataloging in Publication Data

Shelton, Richard, birth date
You can't have everything.

Poems.
I. Title.
PS3569.H39367Y6   811'.5'4   75–9128
ISBN 0–8229–3309–8
ISBN 0–8229–5262–9 pbk.

Acknowledgment is made to the following publications for permission to reprint poems that appear in this book: *The American Scholar, Field, The Goddard Journal, Lillabulero, Madrona, The New York Quarterly, The Paris Review, Pebble, Three Rivers Poetry Journal*, and *Works*.

"As You Were" and "Pomp and Circumstances" were first published in *Antaeus*; "The Monster," in *The Antioch Review*, vol. XXXIII, no. 1; "Behind the Wreckage of My Eyes," "Confession," "Job the Father," and Navajo Song," in *Kayak*, no. 35; "Another Darkness," in *The Ohio Review*; and "The Little Dogs" and "Survival," in *Poetry*.

"Stranger" is reprinted courtesy of *New Mexico Magazine*.
The poem "The Great Gulf," © 1972 The New Yorker Magazine, Inc. The poems "Sonora for Sale," "Comfort," and "The Princes of Exile," © 1973 The New Yorker Magazine, Inc.
"Bad Habits" is reprinted with permission from *The PTA Magazine*, 700 North Rush Street, Chicago, Illinois 60611.

Some of these poems appeared previously in *Among the Stones*, by Richard Shelton, published by Monument Press, 1973, and *Chosen Place*, by Richard Shelton, published by The Best Cellar Press, 1975.

The epigraph on page 1 is from *J. B.*, by Archibald MacLeish, published by Houghton Mifflin Company.

Contents

part 1

POTTER'S FIGURES

Out in the desert in the tombs
Are potter's figures: two of warriors,
Two of worthies, two of camels,
Two of monsters, two of horses.
Ask them why. They will not answer you . . .

—Archibald MacLeish

Excerpts from the Notebook
of the Poet of Santo Tomas

If you live where I come from
and you want to be rich
and beautiful, first get rich.
Then we'll tell you
you are beautiful.
Hell! Settle for that.
You can't have everything.

*

Walk down Main Street at midnight
when the only places open
are two bars in the same block.
Turn the corner and walk past
the homes of the good people
of Santo Tomas. Everybody
will be doing one of three things
rather well: sleeping, drinking,
or the thing we all think we would
do better with somebody else's
husband or wife. And maybe
an angel, like a huge white moth,
will be hovering over each of us.

*

Years ago some desperate
farmer took this land away
from the desert, and every summer
the desert wants it back.
In the heat, everything
stops moving, even the dogs.
All night cicadas drill our teeth.
Water gets scarce
and what little there is
is warm and bitter, but we learn
to drink our liquor straight.

*

New people come here
sometimes, but don't stay long.
I'd like to know what attracts them.
Maybe the need to suffer;
we all have it, like a bird
pecking away inside us
as if inside an egg.
Some people think that if you
suffer enough you'll get to be
better, even noble, but I've lived
here forty years and I get
meaner every day.

*

4

I have nothing to recommend me
except longevity. And hell,
what good is that?
Show me an old man who doesn't
envy every stud he sees
and I'll show you a body
with the undertaker's fingerprints
all over it.

*

Because of the way they dress
it's getting hard to tell
the whores from the female
schoolteachers, which probably
means that whoring isn't
as well paid a profession
as it used to be, what with
all the enthusiastic
amateurs around here.

*

I used to think this bar
was the center of the community
and if I sat here long enough
I'd learn everything worth knowing
about the people of Santo Tomas.
But this afternoon I went
to the funeral of the richest
man in town and watched his two
widows fighting over which of them
would follow his coffin to the grave.
Now I realize that all
significant social events
still take place in church.

*

The earth is moving several ways
at once, but sometimes I wonder
if we are going with it.
And when the drive-in movie
shuts down for the night,
the stars remain over Santo Tomas
like holes in the darkness
through which we see
a cold, enormous light.

*

I don't think death will be
much use to us,
since we've grown accustomed
to using pain for our purposes,
and even love, when we have to.
I think death will arrive
when we have nothing left to use
to get what we want,
or when we no longer want anything,
whichever comes first.

I've learned to wait. Nothing
we want is ever worth
what we go through to get it,
and the difference between what
little we have to offer
and how much we're asked to pay
is life, a kind of debt
we always owe somebody.
I'm in no hurry to pay it.

Stations of the Cross

if you can't make it in Newark
milking the canaries you can
leave your wedding cake

and go to Cleveland Des Moines
or Little Rock if you can't make it
there because of the humidity

you can go to Tucson to drink
the air and live in the sun
if you can't make it in Tucson

because of the heat you can
go to California and wear
dark glasses and if you can't

make it in California you can go
to Hell it isn't far the border
runs right through Los Angeles

Pomp and Circumstances

1

at seventeen she waited for her lover
by the gymnasium while oleander blossoms
fell rotting at her feet

upstairs across the street
someone was playing Malagueña on the piano
he was very good

she was thinking of the reasons
kept from her for years
and all valid

waiting for silent days to arrive
and take her and for nights
like long beaches
which would deliver her wholly to the moon

2

her hands have grown
beyond their reputations
into gloves which fit her like claws

tonight she is trying
to get drunk and not quite making it
never quite making it anymore

it's amazing how things change he says
I came through here years ago
and this was just a dirty
little Mexican town

it still is she says
and don't come back don't you
ever come back

3

dawn slips over the mountains
as if nobody will notice
but the birds give it away

she thinks of the simplicity of birds
who are taught to fly and then know everything
while she must keep on learning
again and again

Prayer to the Virgin in a Cage

Little Mother we are sorry
to keep you in this prison
but if we released you
you would run away

Poor Little Mother
who would care for you
and love you and bring you flowers

the world is very big
and full of evil
and the nights are dark

you would be afraid
with no one to talk to you
or light a small candle for you

and Dear Little Mother do not think
only of yourself your suffering
think also of us
who would we pray to then

Navajo Song

Where one mountain sits on top of another
we turn the basket upside down
and sing a holy song.

>   *We are in great peace.*
>   *We are in great peace.*

It is not true
but it will confuse our enemies,
and none can sing the dead back again.

*

The little bat sits in the last row
with his coat over his head.
Take our pain and put it into the fire.

>   *We are in great peace.*
>   *We are in great peace.*

When you ask for something
you must give something in return,
but none can sing the dead back again.

The Seven Ages of Man

1. *The Age of Miracles*

    returns to a small
    village in Peru

    they recognize him
    at once and rush out
    to meet him singing

    carrying cripples
    and diseased children

    after the ceremony
    they are happier
    than they have ever been

    they proclaim a holiday
    of joy and divide

    his flesh among them
    placing his bones
    carefully like seeds

    in a new grave

2. *The Age of Romance*

    sits on a hill
    and looks toward the sea

    beyond him the surface
    of the water tears light
    into a thousand pieces

and throws them
in all directions

soon he will get up
and return to his house
in the city

he will look out the window
and it will be twilight

darkness will begin to build
its nest under the eaves
this beautiful pain

lasts such a short time
he will say

and so few notice it

3. *The Age of Desire*

walks all night through streets
of a foreign city whose language
he does not speak

his feet are delicate
his boots highly polished

in each lighted window
he sees images of what his life
could be if it were real

he knows exactly what he wants
but cannot find it

every morning he returns
to his small ugly room
takes out a loaded revolver

places it on the table
and writes in his diary

the entry for tomorrow

4. *The Age of Despair*

rides into town
on a crippled horse

his eyes are pale and blue
his eyebrows droop
like twin mustaches

his worn suitcase
is covered with labels

Bombay Marrakesh Rome
Brisbane Tampico Des Moines
Fairbanks La Tierra Eterna

he looks at the muddy
streets and wooden sidewalks

his eyes shift
toward the mountains
he knows this place

is like all the others

5. *The Age of War*

poses like a young man
on his wedding night

his magnificent profile
appears on the coins
of many countries

beneath the mask
his eye sockets are empty

he is older than anyone
but our hearts cannot resist
a man so young and beautiful

and so blind

6. *The Age of Elegance*

arrives and there is
no one to meet him
no porters no taxis

the wind outside
blows and blows

taking one satchel
containing underwear
a clean shirt money

and a pistol he
begins to walk

down a dirt road
toward several small
bumps on the horizon

which he correctly
assumes to be

civilization

7. *The Age of Progress*
   speeds down the freeway
   making history

   evening arrives
   but what can he do
   with such a thing

   nothing exists for him
   unless it is advertised

   the coyote and quail
   did not ask his
   permission to live

   so he carries a gun
   and shoots at close range

   he deals in real estate
   the mountains fear him more
   than they fear an earthquake

   they know the deadly angel
   who troubled the waters

   now troubles the land

As You Were

A waitress with a bluebird
tattooed on her arm
comes to take your order.
You order her to show you
all her birds: the fat
robin on her thigh,
the hummingbird on each
nipple, the bird of paradise.
And when they fly away
you wonder if you are
as capable of trapping
birds as you were.

This is a strange place
full of real trees
sporting fictitious names.
Sacred datura no longer
grows beside the road
and how can you go on
without hallucinations?
The ones you chose,
the ones you paid for.
You want to crawl back
into the old accordion
and be squeezed as you were.

A great decrease of blessings
ripples over you
like debts you will
never pay. Did you read
the words or did they pass
through your eyes as the train
passes through the tunnel,
leaving it empty,
leaving you as you were?

You stand at attention
while the captain screams
as you were, as you were,
but there is no way to go back.

Sleep

There is an old man I dream about every night. He is ugly and his breath stinks. He walks up to me and says, "Drop dead!" I say, "Bug off, old man!" He says, "Drop dead!" I say . . . well, you get the picture. This goes on all night. I wake up every morning exhausted. I guess he sleeps during the day, getting ready for the nightly battle. He never seems to tire of it. I try staying awake to avoid him, but as soon as I slip over the edge, he appears. "Drop dead!" "Bug off, old man!" And on it goes.

Lately I have come to believe he is somebody I know or remember from the past. I look for him all the time. I go to bingo games and stare at each face. I hang around rest homes. Sometimes I wear a white coat and pretend I work there; sometimes I just sneak in and watch television in the lobby among drooping chins and complaining intestines. But I never find him. He is too clever for me. I walk through parks in the afternoon and have begun to frequent certain bars where the dead mingle with the dying and nobody makes distinctions.

And each night he returns. "Drop dead!" he says. "Bug off, old man!" I tell him. It's a helluva way to live. I drink more now than I should, and sometimes it almost works. When he comes he is vague and staggering, and his speech is not clear, but he comes anyway. And sometimes I almost think I recognize that drunken face: eyes like a battlefield after a war and the ruins of what must have been an irresistible smile.

It isn't all bad. I've gotten to know some of the old ones. I kind of enjoy the bingo; it's fun if you win. And they seem to like me. Sometimes during commercials we talk about things. Nothing much, but things. They listen when I tell them about my problem and how tired I am because I don't sleep well. They seem to understand, and nobody else did. I even forget to look for him among them, since it's been so long and I haven't found him.

As a matter of fact, I've kind of settled in with them, I guess. I know it's strange for anyone of my age to spend his afternoons in the park and his evenings watching television in an old folk's home. I could be out dancing tonight if I wanted to, but this is more comfortable, and I have friends here. I couldn't just desert them, could I?

And it's odd, these last few years he doesn't come anymore in my dreams. Lately it's been a young man who bobs in, bright and shiny and kind of friendly, with an irresistible smile, like somebody I knew but can't remember. And he says, "Don't forget me." And I say, "Let me sleep, young man!" And he says, "Sleep, old friend, you have won the battle." And I sleep.

The Monster

I have a singular talent: the ability to make old women cry. Whenever I see one, I say to her, "Something is lost and since it was never here and I have never seen it, I despair of finding it. Please help me! There is no one else for me to turn to."

She begins to search frantically, not knowing for what, and she finds various things. A darning egg, a bus token, a stiffened shoe, a ceramic bird. And she holds these things up to me one by one, saying, "Is this it? Is this?" And each time I shake my head sadly.

Sooner or later she comes upon the one thing she has hidden from herself, the thing she has successfully forgotten. A tiny spoon, a necklace with a broken clasp, a sea shell. And when she finds it, she begins to cry.

Job the Father

I have made my bed in darkness.
Job 17:13

all his children in the same house
and a great wind comes
out of the wilderness

seven sons three daughters
all his eggs in one basket
and a great wind comes

reading the story I am paper
curling to avoid the flame

and no matter what I ask them
the stars say *yes yes yes*
all over the sky

I have but one son all my children
in one place always

and I am still here Lord
in the desert where even my fear
has grown a little courage of its own

saying *take me Lord*
take only me
and I will forgive you everything

Prophecy, Poetry, and the Camel's Nose

He called himself a prophet-poet and was employed in the household of a minor king who ruled one of the small eastern provinces at the edge of the desert. We no longer remember the prophet-poet's name, but we always tell his story to our children, as our fathers told it to us. And while the story is only a legend based on one very old and unreliable document, it is probably true. Certainly it is too bizarre to have been made up.

His duties as a prophet were to foretell the sex of each of the king's unborn children and the outcome of any battle in which the king might wish to engage. As a poet, he was expected to provide a poem for each wedding in the royal family and for other ceremonies and feast days. But his prophecies were always inaccurate, and his poetry was of such little merit that it loses nothing in translation.

In fact, his long poems were so painfully tedious to listeners that the king finally established a decree making it unlawful to read poetry in public, a decree which was received by the people with such overwhelming approval that the prohibition spread to neighboring countries where it has remained in effect to this day. And although it is not for this reason we still remember the prophet-poet, other men have been honored by history for accomplishing less.

Eventually, because of an erroneous prophecy, the king became engaged in a disastrous war with a wild tribe of barbarians to the north. The king's forces were overcome, and the victorious barbarians, whose imaginations were developed only in the areas of violence and torture, entered the palace. Hearing the screams of the captives from his hiding place in the privy, the prophet-poet decided to relinquish his position as factotum to the king. He slipped behind the palisades and escaped on a one-eyed camel —straight into the desert.

It was rumored that beyond the desert lay the sea, and today we know this is true, but in those days no one knew what lay beyond the desert because no one had ever crossed it. And so, having abandoned himself to the desert, the prophet-poet had little hope of survival. Shortly after midday when his small supply of water was gone, he put a pebble in his mouth to allay his thirst. That night when the camel would go no farther, the exhausted traveler dismounted and fell on the ground, remembering only to spit out the pebble so he would not strangle on it in his sleep.

When he woke in the morning, he discovered the camel drinking at a small stream flowing from the sand near where the pebble had fallen. After quenching his thirst from the stream and eating some of the bread and cheese he carried with him, he felt much better and began to consider all the possible and impossible combinations of chance or mischance by which this miracle had occurred. He could come to no conclusion except that the pebble, with which he had been so intimately associated on the previous day, was in some way responsible for the presence of the stream, that it had somehow attracted the water. Then with the boldness and logic characteristic of saints and idiots, he popped the pebble back into his mouth, filled his small waterskin, mounted his camel, and started off again further into the desert.

And it happened exactly as he had expected, as if he were, after all, a true prophet. Each night he dropped the pebble on the ground, and each morning when he woke he found a small stream seeping from the desert floor nearby. He was so pleased that every morning he rode on with great cheer, reciting one or the other of his long poems, the sound of which was only slightly improved by the fact that he carried the precious pebble always in his mouth.

After many days he came to the sea and was rescued by a ship which took him to a distant land. What became of the one-eyed camel we do not know; but we know that the prophet-poet lived in exile long enough to write a thirty-two-volume poem called "The Journey of the Pebble," and that a copy of this poem eventually found its way back to the desert he had crossed.

For within a few weeks of his journey, others also ventured into the desert out of necessities no less desperate than his had been, and soon a group of them discovered the small stream at the spot where he had spent the first night. Then the second stream was discovered, and the third. Within a few years it was known that there were many streams in the desert, each spaced one day's journey from the other, and that the traveler who went from one to the next would be following an erratic line, sometimes veering to the north and sometimes to the south, but leading inevitably to the sea.

Fugitives who escaped from the war-torn eastern provinces settled near these streams and planted date groves and olive trees. The oases they created became small communities which supplied food and shelter to merchant caravans from many lands, for this was the only route to and from the coast. The streams were expanded and directed into systems of canals which furnished water for miles of farmlands, vineyards, and groves. Nor have the people of these cities ever engaged in war, since it has always been obvious that each city is merely a link in a chain stretching across the desert from the inland provinces to the sea, and that if trade between any two of the cities should fail, the chain would be broken and they would all perish.

It is not beyond the bounds of modesty to say that we who live in the Cities of the Pebble are blessed above others. Not only have we been permitted to live in peace, but we have learned much from the travelers who follow the road past our doors. In order to trade, we have learned many languages, and our schools are often models for schools in other lands. Our craftsmen and artists are famous throughout the world. We have developed cotton of the finest quality known to man, and our fabric dyes, made from certain desert plants which grow nowhere else, are quite literally worth their weight in gold.

And we do not consider it a blot on our record that we have produced no great prophets or poets. Prophets sometimes visit our cities but never stay very long since no one pays the slightest attention to them. They soon decide that if they are going to be without honor anyway, they might as well go home. As for poets, our law which does not permit poetry to be read aloud in public is probably the reason why so few of our citizens attempt to follow that vocation. And those poets who pass through our cities, upon finding they will not be able to perform before audiences, usually leave quickly.

We accept the name "Cities of the Pebble" as the consequence of poetic error and because it has been handed down for many generations. But we, who have lived all our lives surrounded by the desert, know that a camel—even a one-eyed camel—can smell water many miles away. And we know that if given his head in the desert, a camel will lead the traveler to a place, and there are such places, where water lies very near the surface, although it cannot be detected by men. We also know that a camel will dig with his strong toes all night if necessary to reach the underground stream which his infallible nose has told him is there. So we believe in neither prophecy nor poetry, but place our trust in our own hard work and the noses of our camels.

Part 2

CONFESSIONS

We are time and it is not the years
that pass but we ourselves.

—Octavio Paz

Disintegration

the day after you left
things began to break down
as if they were trying
to tell me something

first the cooler died
without warning
and the dogs accused me
of causing the heat

then it rained
and the roof leaked
so I waded through empty rooms
learning that a mop
speaks only to a bucket
and a bucket speaks to no one

this morning
after the dishwasher drowned
in its own soapy water
all the eggs
fell out of the refrigerator
and lay on the floor
staring up at me
with their broken eyes

now I feel the old
pain in my hip
which has returned and moved in
to take your place

soon the valves of my body
will begin to falter
the intricate webs
of my muscles will unweave
while my teeth slowly loosen
and the lines
on my face go astray

but I would have been
no use without you anyway
what good is one shoe

Youth

is the ability to be
single-minded as water caressing a stone
and ambidextrous as the wind
ringing all its bells
at the same time

but tomorrow is over
so what can I do with today
coming as it does at the wrong time
for everybody including me

who wasted my youth in celibacy
hard work and studies
and now find myself
turning to riotous living in vain

what does the water feel
just as it gets to the edge and decides
to go down
what does the wind have to say
about the direction it is blowing

we do not choose what we must have
but we must have it anyway
and if we cannot get it
we will die

I do not know what happens after that
to our transparent lives
or to the wreckage
our lack of dreams creates

when I tell the truth
there is so little to say

At Forty

I don't remember
where I was going
or how I got here
except for a few moments
in the womb of a train at night

outside the window a moon
and inside a sound
so steady it seemed like silence

it's too late I know
but I keep thinking it will
get earlier I will start
getting younger slowly
and this time doing it backwards
I will do it right

and finally I will
grow smaller and become
a good wise child at last

November 1st

last night
the daughters of ignorance
coupled with the sons of despair
in cars parked by a ruined river
while dreams were finding their way home
in the dark
old dreams
staying on old roads
new dreams falling into ditches

troops were being withdrawn
from one battlefield to another
and the President was about to be reelected
because he had killed more than any other
and was the best man for the job
and because he wears a mask
on the back of his head
smiling
and because he lives
where the hair of a telescopic sight
crosses its target

but today is the day of the dead
so this morning I placed at the feet
of unfinished statues the scars I have salvaged
it's my way of protesting

now I sit in a bar
with the bartender and the cockroaches
pretending I am here on a visit
when I know this is home

like a man with no legs
trying to cross them

Behind the Wreckage of My Eyes

my body no longer responds
as well as it did
to its own desires

each hair is leaving my head
like a migratory bird
on its last journey

what I wanted most
was not to be wise or good
but to be beautiful

and I was never beautiful
not even for a moment
or in the dark

I had to say that
in order to say this

first I must learn
to live with it
then I must live with it

and I can't blame anyone
not even myself

Bad Habits

how could I leave you behind
old friends
since I am going nowhere

here is good and there is evil
and again I fall like a drunk
between two stools

of all the things I have
I cherish most
what no one else would want

Climbing

the age of consent
is a sad story
and I don't want to hear about it

I feel very old tonight
almost beyond the point
where youth and beauty can hurt me

but the broken moon
hangs out there
like half a golden egg
not willing to give itself
for nothing
while the big dipper pours
huge streams of darkness over us

light of my life
wherever you flicker
look down on my ruined face
it has come of age

at last I know what to do
and where to go to do it
so let them envy me
those who have not yet
achieved destruction

I know about the faulty
rung in the ladder
and I am climbing
fast as I can

The Little Dogs

La vida no vale nada.

It is the season of rain. I am
lonely and afraid in a dark land,
riding the bus of three stars
and wondering how long my bones
will nestle in their sockets. Why
did I come here? Where am I going
while the moon advances toward me
like a lopsided egg, and the little
dogs of Mexico are howling?

The road opens a scarred hand
flooded with obsidian, but the driver
is an artist inspired by danger.
We will arrive perhaps tomorrow,
blinking among the artificial flowers
and Coca-Colas. Tonight we move
against the stars, toward the interior,
while our voices sleep beside us,
curled in wooden bowls.

We come to La Piedad but it is closed.
The only thing with lights on
is a cross on the hill. Two women
sleep on the church steps; their mouths
are empty dice cups. La Piedad is moist
and warm and smells like human shit.
I would settle for any change
in weather and talk to a bicycle
if it spoke English.

A cloud's black paw attacks the moon
which shatters, falling and becoming
thousands of golden fish in the Rio Lerma.
They swim beside us. The road lies down
and dies young of natural causes.
At dawn the water turns brown, the fish
sink. We descend into the valley
of the lion's tooth, the monkey's
thumb, the jackal's smile.

When the sun rises, green corn
shoots like fire from volcanic soil.
We roll into a village marketplace
crowded with those who have come to sell
what others have come to buy.
As I step down from the bus of three
stars, the earth shifts to the left,
and clouds of dust rise above the houses.
This must be where I was going.

Walls are falling around us. Children
stare at me and scream as if I
had brought disaster. Those who
were promised nothing have arrived
to claim it. Little dogs are everywhere.
They know I have come a long way
and cannot go back, that I have come
to sell myself, and they know
how much will be offered.

Hotel Eldorado

Where can it be—
This land of Eldorado?
Edgar Allen Poe

at the hour of birth and death
between the light's first
tentative movements and sunrise
the gulls are beginning to cry
and the women who sell
shawls on the beach
are sorting and folding
their goods as if they were
preparing for a long journey

dawn calls our names
so softly it expects no answer
and I wake beside you
on a mattress
stained by the sweat
of younger more competent lovers

soon today will arrive with its
new resolve and its tendencies
toward an old horizon

the dark sea will turn gold
each grain of sand
will hold up its tiny
translucent windows to the sun
and the flowers in the garden
will open to any trespasser

but the tide has already
turned and gone away
not having found what it wanted

From a Room

Hidden in the nest of its cord
a telephone is ringing.
The dark room smells of cheap perfume.
It is the orange trees
blooming outside the windows.
I cannot find the telephone.

In its nest of dark windows
the room is hidden. A telephone
blooms in the cheap orange trees.
I cannot find the perfumed
cord, the hidden ringing.

Perfume is ringing in a nest
of hidden telephones.
I cannot find the room,
the dark cord out the window,
the ringing orange trees.

The room smells of cheap telephones.
The dark perfume is ringing.
The cord blooms. I cannot find
the hidden windows in the orange trees.

Sonora for Sale

this is the land of gods in exile
they are fragile and without pride
they require no worshipers

we come down a white road in the moonlight
dragging our feet like innocents
to find the guilty already arrived
and in possession of everything

we see the stars as they were years ago
but for us it is the future
they warn us too late

we are here we cannot turn back
soon we hold out our hands
full of money
this is the desert
it is all we have left to destroy

Letter to a Dead Father

Five years since you died and I am
better than I was when you were living.
The years have not been wasted.
I have heard the harsh voices
of desert birds who cannot sing.
Sometimes I touched the membrane
between violence and desire
and watched it vibrate.
I learned that a man
who travels in circles
never arrives at exactly the same place.

If you could see me now
side-stepping triumph and disaster,
still waiting for you to say *my son*
my beloved son. If you could only see
me now, you would know I am stronger.

Death was the poorest subterfuge
you ever managed, but it was permanent.
Do you see now that fathers
who cannot love their sons
have sons who cannot love?
It was not your fault
and it was not mine. I needed
your love but I recovered without it.
Now I no longer need anything.

The Great Gulf

Between us and you there is a
great gulf fixed: so that they
which would pass from hence to you
cannot; neither can they pass to us,
that would come from thence.

Luke 16:26

1

At night when each dark shape in the desert
glows in the light of its own penumbra
I take the road by one white hand
and lead it to a deep arroyo, a dry wash
in which the river lives when it is home.
Stones remain where the water dropped them
and beneath them aged scorpions sleep
in small hotels with no view at all.
The sand is cool. I wonder if the river
will be here when I need to drown.

2

We choose from what is available and fall
in love: anchorites with spiders, sailors
with each other; the bleeding foot
returns to embrace the shattered glass;
the overdose goes in search of an addict;
and those who are too much afraid
fall in love with their fear.

3

I was broken by love but I was
so well repaired I can pass for anybody,
standing here where a river used to be.
In one hand my prayers, in the other the answers,
with a great gulf fixed between them.

To get here I dragged my shadow
over sharp stones and felt its cuts
and bruises. But the river was dry.

Oh Jesus Christ
and all my fingers losing their rings!
What will become of me when I offer
my soul to the Devil and he doesn't
want it? What will I do
when there is no one left to betray?

Confession

We are all here: the voyeur
with an eye at each fingertip,
the blackmailer with a dimple
in the palm of each hand,
the professional with his knife,
the amateur with his can opener,
the young rapist in tennis shoes,
the cat who dips into the fishbowl,
and the wolf who comes to the door.

It begins slowly. We are shy.
At last from the back of the room
one murmurs, *Lord, I have sinned,*
and another, *Lord, I am a sinner.*
Those who denied their names
at the door begin to reclaim them,
recounting tiny cruelties at first,
then mutilations and murders.

Soon we tell the sins we dreamed of
but never committed and the sins
of others. We implicate our enemies,
our friends, our children, anyone.
We are all shouting at once
into microphones which wither
like tulips, and our voices rise
as an odor which darkens the ceiling.

I forced him to watch while I . . .
I wrapped the child up and . . .
I told her enough to make sure . . .

A thousand pardons circle above us,
screaming for flesh, while guilt
beats itself to death on the windows.
And little by little we have
nothing left to say. We lean back
exhausted and wonder why the best
years of our lives were not as good
as we remember them nor as bad
as they seemed at the time.

And now we return our purified
selves to the capable hands
of politicians, sheriffs, and judges,
where each of us will be done
and done and done like a door.

part 3

EXILES

We are the children of our landscape; it
dictates behaviour and even thought in the
measure to which we are responsive to it.

—Lawrence Durrell

Doing Without

If I can bear your laughter, as you and your friends pass by in search of further pleasures, forgive me my silence. It indicates neither envy nor contempt. I am a Stoic in a land of Epicureans. I know your life is not all pleasure, just as I know there are two choices and both are valid. We can enjoy the strokes and take the licks that go with them, or we can do without. Any other path will lead to misery.

A good case can be made for doing without. Think of it not as a lack of companionship and pleasure, but as a lack of complicity and disappointment. And there will always be animals. When they act as if they love you, for that moment at least, they love you. Nor will you find yourself by traveling from place to place. Instead, you will find other travelers, each avoiding himself. Why not stay in one place and wait? It may take years, but so does travel.

First you must escape. When you hear someone calling your name, and there will be someone calling your name, look carefully in the wrong direction and walk on. Move into a small house at the outskirts of a town like Ely, Nevada. Live alone. Be courteous but distant to everyone you meet. Each of them will make up a story to explain your presence, and each will believe his own story.

Years later, while thin bodies of smoke rise above houses on the mountain, and snow is forgiving the ugly for its ugliness, the beautiful for its beauty, there will be long mornings of rapture when you can't remember your name. Such happiness can be endured if it is earned, and it is earned by doing without.

Another Darkness

when I stay awake all night
for whatever purpose
morning accuses me
of a new understanding of absence

another dawn arrives
as if I had been waiting for it
and the mountains approach
looking blue and innocent
trying to convince me
they were standing there all the time
when I know they were somewhere else
staring into another darkness

tiny crystals of ice
form while I'm not looking and depart
before I can tell them goodby
how difficult
to live on such a schedule

darkness
place without maps
place without encumbrances
can I lay claim to your country
whose trees bear no initials

Absence Cold and Hunger

these are the poor processes
it takes to make a winter
and some of us enjoy a good
funeral more than anything

but the wind comes to the window
to deliver its message quickly
and go away in search of an empty
place for its homeless children

and the grass under the snow
cares nothing for our secrets
since it is dying
with secrets of its own

Comfort

do not worry
the snow will melt
the roads will again be passable
these delays are temporary
those who left you will come back

the spilled milk will be replaced
and the doll's missing blue eye
will be sewn on in exactly the right place

the hand of darkness you held all night
which slipped from you at dawn
will come over the horizon
reaching for your hand
and the pain will return

Drought

when the days pass at a distance
hot and dry and each one
like the last
and even the cactus suffers
from lack of water

some of us keep saying
look I have nothing to say
and others keep saying
anything anything anything

how difficult it is
to accept silence
the only child we have left
after truth has been run out of town
and music is found dead

Now

a time of peace
comes like rain to the desert
after a long drought
giving itself to thirsty birds
and in desert towns giving itself
to every dusty house and street

rain
how could we have
lived so long without you
your tiny fingers on our shoulders
on our faces

rain rain
the doors of our cages are open
but we cannot leave
we are trying to say *wait*
we are trying to say *there is still time*
but we know it is only now
in a different costume
and it is too late

Survival

For Susan North

1

In April summer arrives
facedown. The sun is cruel
but not as cruel as the moon
whose mad face offers comfort.
To be comforted by such a moon
is to walk barefoot through groves
of crippling cholla, scourged
by ocotillo, and crouch all night
in a dry arroyo, howling
like a coyote in search of love.

2

A chaparral hen nests
in the palo verde, alert and still.
Her mate watches from the false
nest they have built to fool
their enemies. Tonight a coyote
is a dark haze five feet
below them. They do not move
or blink their eyes. A rabbit
screams. The glowing shadow
moves past with something dripping
from its mouth. Another shadow stops
to lick the stones, then follows.

3

Three months without rain.
Crazed with thirst, the quail
peck at bits of clear glass
beside the road. Coyotes
and the great cats can quench
their thirst with blood, but where
can the deer find water? What
nourishes the lichen on these stones?

Nature at the mercy of nature,
and man without mercy, the nature
of man. I am secondary
among the primary sources, trying
to save myself from love and other
dangers, trying to hold still.

4

Watched closely by the birds,
I gather the things a man needs
to build his strange nest:
stones for a wall, sand
for mortar, the ribs of dead
saguaros for a roof. A dry
country is for those who choose it,
for those who are fragile
and beat down by such gentle rain.

Today a hot wind wrung me dry.
It died at sunset. Now the road
is white as lime and the desert bleaches
under the moon, all bone and shadow,
the floor of a star-filled sea.

Comfort me with anything but the moon:
salt for a cracked lip, an old
shirt which has lost my shape
but remembers my odor. I know
where my edges are, where I cease
and the desert night begins.

I never broke the rules; the rules
broke me. If I wear protective
coloring, the costume of survival,
it is because I was not equipped
with sharp enough teeth. I have
seen the gods and they are ruthless.

The Future

bright bird with one wing
flying in circles over the place
where morning gets up
stiff from having slept
all night on the damp ground

tomorrow has already happened
how fortunate we are
that we can't remember it

Vespers

it is evening
and birds are taking
daylight home with them
leaving me to manage as best I can
with the moon the stars
and the inner light
great euphemism for darkness

this is the desert where I learned
about suffering how it
goes on until the last
possible moment and beyond

I am one of many
who survive in dangerous places
a gentle minority capable of violence
to themselves
the hidden the hiding
and those who live at a distance
avoiding neighbors and without friends

we climbed the walls
and discovered only the ceiling
we studied suicide and flunked the course
now each remains in his own desert
stuffing bottles with messages
and waiting for someone
to build the sea

love comes to us as salt
in search of a wound
or as a thorn moving toward the flesh
for which it was intended

we are afraid to be touched
by the intricate motors of hands
afraid to be looked at
and tonight I pray for us
to whatever god is available

may each of us be permitted
to create out of darkness and loneliness
as the world was created
that part of himself which is missing
and if we fail in this and go to the dogs
may the dogs accept us

Dry Season

1

some years the birds
fly south for the winter
and there isn't any

trees beckon to them
but they fly into the desert
which has had no autumn rain

it is late October in a dry season
the coyotes are warming up
for a night of unearthly music
and the moon hangs
by its horns
above the Santa Ritas

I am trying to say something
about my life
in a dry season
while thirsty birds sleep
with their heads under their wings
and coyotes chant vanity
vanity vanity

2

when a man loves the desert
he loves it
as he loves a woman

at first in spite of
her imperfections
and later because of them

3

all day I lifted stones
and fitted them into a wall
carrying each one carefully
walking on my heels
like a woman with child

the wall will stand
perhaps five years
before the stones leave me

when they have made
their journeys down slopes
and into deep arroyos
I will slip out and find them
scarred and chipped
in the moonlight
and bring them home

4

there is a bird
who follows me
curious to know what I am doing
and why should he fear me
when he kills rattlesnakes
and outruns coyotes

there is a spider
who struggles so hard
to escape the embrace
of his huge lovesick mate
that he dies of exhaustion

there is a toad
who digs his way six feet up
toward the desert rain
and when he arrives
bleats like a lamb

5

I have chosen this place
and given it a name
it is called my place

a place without subtlety
where morning light
is unfiltered by leaves and the wind
blows unhampered by leaves

where sunlight hurls itself down
as if each day
would be followed by two nights

sunlight which pierces
the closed eyelid
and impales the eye

and after a day heavy with heat
in which to be empty-handed
is burden enough
the sudden vacuum of dry cold

6

now while the moon pulls darkness
toward a place where somebody
must need it more than I do

and new stones
are struggling slowly
to the surface
I wait with the chollas
who stand under the shelter
of their dangerous long blond hair
and watch for rain

7

I who was promised
little by men
have waited for it gone without
in order to have it
and finally it arrives
as a blessing

place I have chosen
where I will not pay tribute
to those from whom
I learned the most

if they want it they must
steal it from me as I
stole their knowledge from them

place I have chosen
where exile is home

thicken my roots and extend them
toward secret compartments
of dark water
which will nurture me
that I might live
a life without explanation
in all the books of men

The Stones

I love to go out on summer nights and watch the stones grow. I think they grow better here in the desert, where it is warm and dry, than almost anywhere. Or perhaps it is only that the young ones are more active here.

Young stones tend to move about more than their elders consider good for them. Most young stones have a secret desire which their parents had before them but have forgotten ages ago. And because this desire involves water, it is never mentioned. The older stones disapprove of water and say, "Water is a gadfly who never stays in one place long enough to learn anything." But the young stones try to work themselves into a position, slowly and without their elders noticing it, in which a sizable stream of water during a summer storm might catch them broadside and unknowing, so to speak, and push them along over a slope or down an arroyo. In spite of the danger this involves, they want to travel and see something of the world and settle in a new place, far from home, where they can raise their own dynasties away from the domination of their parents.

And although family ties are very strong among stones, many of the more daring young ones have succeeded; and they carry scars to prove to their children that they once went on a journey, helter-skelter and high water, and traveled perhaps fifteen feet, an incredible distance. As they grow older, they cease to brag about such clandestine adventures.

It is true that old stones get to be very conservative. They consider all movement either dangerous or downright sinful. They remain comfortably where they are and often get fat. Fatness, as a matter of fact, is a mark of distinction.

And on summer nights, after the young stones are asleep, the elders turn to a serious and frightening subject—the moon, which is always spoken of in whispers. "See how it glows and whips across the sky, always changing its shape," one says. And another says, "Feel how it pulls at us, urging us to follow." And a third whispers, "It is a stone gone mad."

One More Time

*And he took the blind man by the hand,
and led him out of the town; and when
he had spit on his eyes, and put his
hands upon him, he asked him if he saw
ought. And he looked up, and said, I
see men as trees, walking.*

Mark 8:23–24

with my hat on backwards
to salute the sun
which rises behind me

with my incredible consistencies
a shoebox full of cloves and absences
and an anguished letter from my friend
the misunderstood flute
I am moving on

wearing time thin on my shoulders
a little naked hope and not enough
hair to cover my head

I am moving on
with the dentist's bill in my mouth
my teeth in my pocket
and my ticket
in the coat I left in the closet

with the pain in my hip
like a splintered leg I have walked on
so long I know every tooth
in the bone
with my bottle of whiskey and the pain
like a baby I drug and rock
in its cradle all night
saying for God's sake
go to sleep

with the ghost of the father I loved
who could not love me
now holding my hand

and a good woman who was foolish enough
to take me and keep me
not out of charity
but out of her still unsatisfied need
I have survived

I trusted the blind possibilities
and we groped our way
expecting no miracles no
undeserved spittle of Christ

but if it were offered
I would take the journey again
out of darkness through darkness
into darkness
if it were offered
I would take the same journey again

I Have No Wings

but since I have feet I can walk
since I can walk I will arrive
and when I arrive the place will be there

if there are stairs I will climb
if there is water I will swim
if there are words I will speak

when I am desired I will be chosen
when I am chosen I will take my place
when no one is near me I will be alone

a tired man carries only himself
a frightened man carries himself and his shadow
a vicious man carries the weight
of all he would harm

a loud voice is a stranger in any land
if there is silence let me guard it
a low voice rules its own country
if there is love let me hold it
a small room is enough to contain me
if there is hope let me give it a home

Camino Real

each makes his path
his small path

quickly overgrown
but leading him slowly
to where he is going

which is not
where he is planning to go

and when the last vine
or bamboo is cut
he emerges into a clearing

each into a different
clearing

where some are met
by cannibals some by lovers
some by friends

and some by nothing
except a clearing

a sky with stars at night
and by day an unexpected
view of the next hill

which is reason enough
for the long journey
more than reason enough

Wonders of the World

light is a vehicle for shadows
darkness brings only itself

mountains and continents
rising falling
the earth breathes slowly

the river always moving on
the sea always trying to get out

it is cold and they are naked
but the trees catch snow
in their hands

the rain in all its moods
still anonymous

the star in the apple
the nest in the pomegranate
the maze in the onion

Dear Life

if I use my imagination
I can create a river
where I can fish
swim or drown myself
there are always choices

after I have eaten a bad meal
I do not demand my hunger back
nor do I expect the night
to be less cold
because I lack a coat

pain is a room I measure
each time I am in it
and each time I leave
I forget its dimensions

the wind blows over the desert
telling me nothing
but when I forget the force
to which broken stones complain
I will be lost

when I cannot feel the vine's
need to hold onto something
or when I am happy
only in the presence of others
I will be lost

to the God of Joy
or the God of Sadness
I could tell everything
and each would accept my story
and claim me for his own

but to the God of Remorse
I have nothing to say
and no time to say it

I am holding on for dear life
as my chariot rolls
into the future
faster than I would have thought
possible on its square
wooden wheels

Stranger

do not be afraid
of the emptiness around you.
If you remain here,
your eyes will grow accustomed
to desert light.

Then you will be able
to distinguish between seasons.
You will begin to see
the citizens of this country
and realize you are not alone.

As each sun rolls over you
on its journey west,
you will grow
quieter with listening
until you can hear the dry
whispers of scorpions,
and the mountains grinding
against one another with desire.

The cloudless sky
will send all shadows
to places of refuge, but you will
live on the head of a pin
where your needs are balanced
and night comes as a knife
so sharp you feel no pain
but there is a new scar
every morning.

If you give the scars a home
and cherish them,
you will become silent
and worthy of exile, and beautiful
beyond all witnessing.

Local Knowledge

For Michael Hogan

on December nights
when the rain we needed months ago
is still far off and the wind
gropes through the desert
in search of any tree to hold it

those who live here all year round
listen to the irresistible
voice of loneliness
and want only to be left alone

local knowledge is to live in a place
and know the place
however barren

some kinds of damage
provide their own defense
and we who stay in the ruins
are secure against enemies and friends

if you should see one of us
in the distance as your caravan passes
and if he is ragged and gesturing
do not be mistaken

he is not gesturing for rescue
he is shouting *go away*

The Princes of Exile

stand near the gates of the desert
and watch for travelers who pass by.
When they see a familiar face
they turn aside and remain at a distance.
Instead of the music of home they hear
a foreign wind singing
to trees which bear no leaves.

The Princes of Exile move
through languages and are refracted,
dragging their crippled shadows
beneath an alien sun. They wear
masks of greeting. When they
close their eyes, no one can see them.

The Princes of Exile pray
for sleep and that each day
will be shorter than the last.
They go to bed with the passionate
daughters of strangers and are unsatisfied.
They lie awake trying to name
stars they do not recognize.

When a traveler crosses the border
between foreign countries,
he shifts a burden from one hand
to the other. When he crosses
the border into his own land,
he removes a pebble from his shoe.

The Princes of Sacrifice return
as rain in a drought year.
The Princes of War return
as sores on the faces of politicians.
The Princes of Betrayal return
impaled on the swords of their friends.
But the Princes of Exile never return.

Whatever Became of Me

1

because the moon comes
straight up from the mountain
like the hidden possibility of madness
escaped for everyone to see

and the wandering stars
who are said to rule our lives
wander on in darkness

I feel a need to lie down among the stones
and caress any of them
who have survived

2

I always looked for what I wanted
in the wrong places
until the desert
taught me to want what I found

now on summer nights
I sit in the garden
where it is hot and dry
and young stones grow like weeds

when the moon turns
a mad white face upon me
having nothing to offer I hold up
my empty hands
it is so easy to be happy

3

this morning a woodpecker woke me
practicing on his drum
and all afternoon cicadas rang
like the telephones I haven't answered

I am what has become of me
a man who lives in the desert

where coyotes wail more skillfully
than hired mourners
at the funeral of an Eastern king

where every night the stars
whose light I have not earned
and will never deserve
return as if to keep a promise

and even the rain
when it falls is coming home

Adonis, *The Blood of Adonis*
Jack Anderson, *The Invention of New Jersey*
Jon Anderson, *Death & Friends*
Jon Anderson, *In Sepia*
Jon Anderson, *Looking for Jonathan*
John Balaban, *After Our War*
Gerald W. Barrax, *Another Kind of Rain*
Michael Culross, *The Lost Heroes*
Fazıl Hüsnü Dağlarca, *Selected Poems*
James Den Boer, *Learning the Way*
James Den Boer, *Trying to Come Apart*
Norman Dubie, *Alehouse Sonnets*
Norman Dubie, *In the Dead of the Night*
Odysseus Elytis, *The Axion Esti*
John Engels, *The Homer Mitchell Place*
John Engels, *Signals from the Safety Coffin*
Abbie Huston Evans, *Collected Poems*
Brendan Galvin, *No Time for Good Reasons*
Gary Gildner, *Digging for Indians*
Gary Gildner, *First Practice*
Gary Gildner, *Nails*
Michael S. Harper, *Dear John, Dear Coltrane*
Michael S. Harper, *Song: I Want a Witness*
Samuel Hazo, *Blood Rights*
Samuel Hazo, *Once for the Last Bandit: New and Previous Poems*
Samuel Hazo, *Quartered*
Gwen Head, *Special Effects*
Shirley Kaufman, *The Floor Keeps Turning*
Shirley Kaufman, *Gold Country*
Abba Kovner, *A Canopy in the Desert*
Larry Levis, *Wrecking Crew*
Tom Lowenstein, tr., *Eskimo Poems from Canada and Greenland*
Archibald MacLeish, *The Great American Fourth of July Parade*
Judith Minty, *Lake Songs and Other Fears*
James Moore, *The New Body*

Carol Muske, *Camouflage*
Thomas Rabbitt, *Exile*
Belle Randall, *101 Different Ways of Playing Solitaire and Other Poems*
Ed Roberson, *Etai-Eken*
Ed Roberson, *When Thy King Is A Boy*
Dennis Scott, *Uncle Time*
Herbert Scott, *Disguises*
Richard Shelton, *Of All the Dirty Words*
Richard Shelton, *The Tattooed Desert*
Richard Shelton, *You Can't Have Everything*
David Steingass, *American Handbook*
David Steingass, *Body Compass*
Tomas Tranströmer, *Windows & Stones: Selected Poems*
Alberta T. Turner, *Learning to Count*
Marc Weber, *48 Small Poems*
David P. Young, *Sweating Out the Winter*

COLOPHON

This book was set in Palatino, a typeface designed by Hermann Zapf and cut into type by many foundries. The version used here is the Linotype one, which has been set by Heritage Printers, Inc. The design of the book is by Gary Gore.